Gothic Dreams

Zombies

Fantasy Art, Fiction and the Movies

Publisher and Creative Director: Nick Wells
Senior Project Editor: Catherine Taylor
Picture Research: Catherine Taylor
Art Director: Mike Spender
Layout Design: Jane Ashley

Special thanks to: Emma Chafer and Esme Chapman,
and the artists who allowed us to reproduce their work.

FLAME TREE PUBLISHING
Crabtree Hall, Crabtree Lane
Fulham, London SW6 6TY
United Kingdom

www.flametreepublishing.com

First published 2013

15 17 16 14
3 5 7 9 10 8 6 4 2

A CIP record for this book is available from the British Library upon request.

Hardback ISBN: 978-0-85775-993-1
Paperback ISBN: 978-1-78361-266-6

Printed in China

Gothic Dreams

Zombies

Fantasy Art, Fiction and the Movies

RUSS THORNE

Foreword by Rosie Fletcher

FLAME TREE
PUBLISHING

MONROEVILLE
MALL

Contents

Foreword

The great thing about zombies is that they're just so flexible. A stumbling reminder of the inevitability of death, a symbol of the faceless masses... zombies are the perfect vessels to project onto. Used to explore themes of slavery and civil rights, capitalism, consumerism, communism, terrorism and, recently, more personal concerns of loneliness and isolation, the undead shuffle along with the times.

I fell in love with zombies with George Romero's 1968 masterpiece *Night Of The Living Dead* – terrifying and subversive, it marks the template for the modern zombie. I've even been a zombie myself – I staggered around South London with a gaping hole in my cheek and some spectacular oozing welts as an extra in the low-budget Brit horror *Colin*, a movie which uses zombification as a metaphor for lost love and was at the forefront of a trend for exploring the world from a zombie's point of view. I've thoroughly enjoyed *In The Flesh* and *The Returned* on television, which take this idea even further, with rehabilitated zombies who can function as normal members of society. More than anything these new metamorphoses go to prove that the zombie genre has plenty of life left.

In these pages you'll find a journey through zombie history from Haitian drones to Romero's undead, Danny Boyle's infected to *Warm Bodies*' zombie Romeo. It's an exploration of the walking dead in art, culture, media and music. There's even a guide to events where you can become a zombie yourself – I'd wholeheartedly recommend it! After all – funny or scary, romantic or moving, zombies just won't stay dead.

Rosie Fletcher, Associate Editor, *Total Film*

© aaron sims

Pleased to Eat You: Introducing the Zombie

You never forget your first zombie.

There are lots of ways to encounter them, but that first meeting tends to leave an impression. It might be late at night, watching a movie and seeing those vacant eyes, hearing those shuffling steps for the first time; it might be in the pages of a horror novel; or it might be watching the world's most celebrated music video and seeing Michael Jackson do *that* dance. But wherever and whenever you meet zombie zero, they leave a lasting impression.

This book is a celebration and investigation of all things living dead. They don't move quickly, so zombies have perhaps taken more time than other creatures to really work their way to the top of the heap. We'll stagger with them as they rise from shameful roots on slave plantations, follow them through eras of supernatural scares and space age shocks, revel in the zombie renaissance of the 1960s and, finally, glory in the global apocalypse that the early-twenty-first century walking dead are bringing to our lives.

Along the way we'll meet memorable zombie characters and look at just why zombies are so appealing. We'll even find some zombie music to listen to while we're at it. So nut up, shut up, buckle up and get ready to meet Z. And try not to get red on you.

'I can't really make
fun of zombies.
They're not liars.
They're not cheats.'

George A. Romero

The Rise of the Zombie

They may seem to be everywhere now, but the 'modern' incarnation of the zombie has only been with us since the 1960s, courtesy of George A. Romero's 1968 *Night of the Living Dead* (see page 33). However, they did exist in a different form before that and, of course, ideas of the resurrection of the dead have been with us for centuries.

Ghosts, vampires, ghouls … all have taken their place in the pantheon of faith and folklore. In Great Britain's High Middle Ages (1000–1299 AD) stories of 'revenants' were commonplace, involving the dead returning to walk the Earth, often to right some wrong done to them in life; across the world, Chinese folklore speaks of the *jiangshi*, animated corpses who move with a hopping gait. Wander through Norse mythology and you'll encounter the *draugr*, undead beings guarding burial hordes and with an unfortunate taste for blood and flesh; similarly ancient Arabian folklore features the ghoul (or *ghul*), a kind of demonic undead creature.

Clearly, the concept of the walking dead has been around for as long as we have. However, to find the roots of the zombie we need to look to Haiti, and the practice of voodoo.

Voodoo Mild

If ever a religion was maligned and misunderstood, it's voodoo – or more accurately, *voudou*. A synthesis of West African beliefs and Catholicism, it developed in eighteenth-century

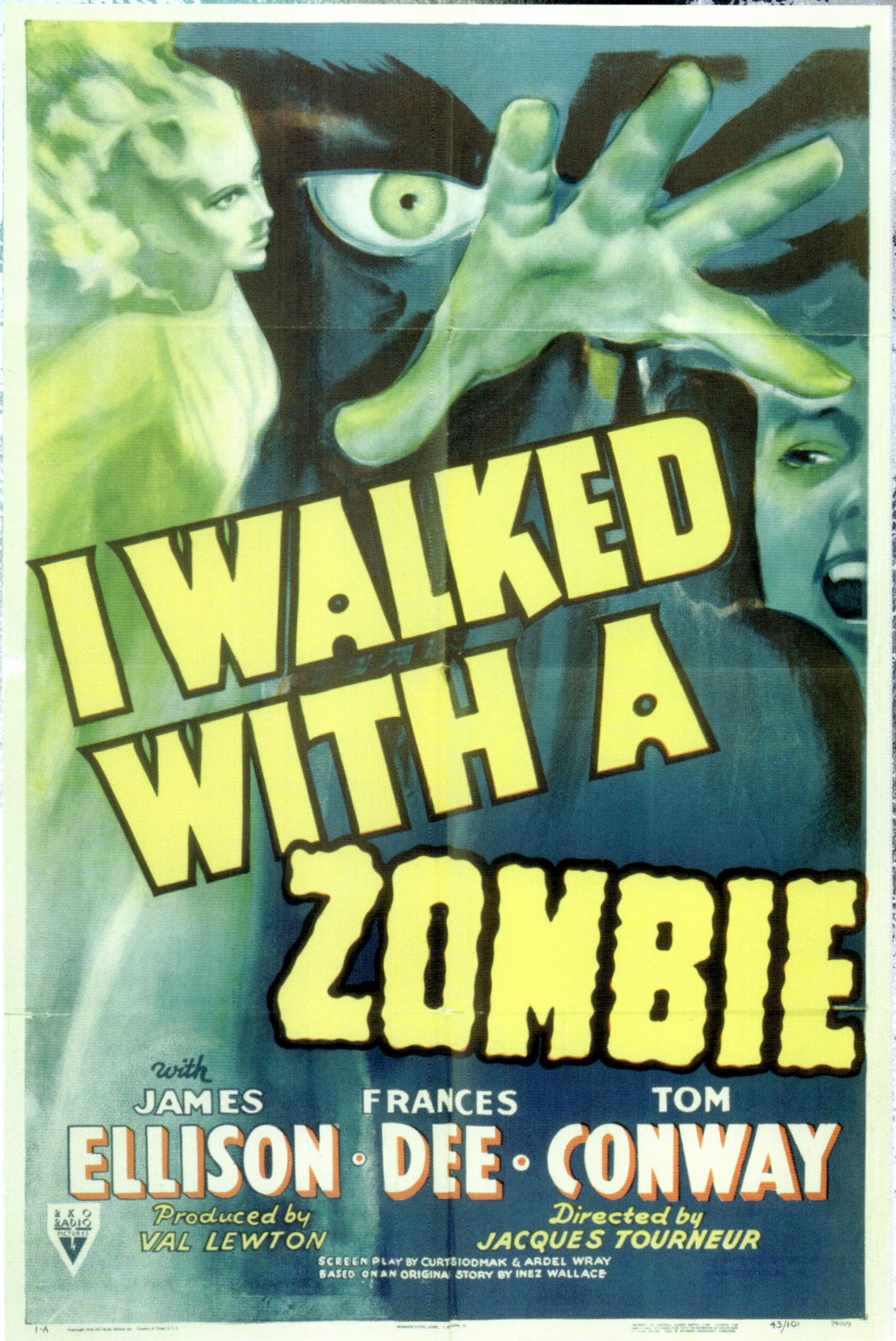

I WALKED WITH A ZOMBIE
with
JAMES ELLISON · FRANCES DEE · TOM CONWAY
Produced by VAL LEWTON
Directed by JACQUES TOURNEUR
SCREEN PLAY BY CURT SIODMAK & ARDEL WRAY
BASED ON AN ORIGINAL STORY BY INEZ WALLACE

'It would not be easy to believe that the corpses of the dead should sally from their graves, did not frequent examples, occurring in our own times, suffice to establish this fact.'

William of Newburgh, writing in the 1190s

slave colonies (such as St Dominique and, later, Haiti) as authorities attempted to stamp out the native faiths of their African slaves and force Christianity upon them. The result was a blend of many faiths and a central belief in a supreme being, *Bondyè*.

While *Bondyè* is central to voudou, what isn't is a cult of the zombie (pincushion voodoo dolls as a tool of vengeance are a Hollywood invention, too), as it's primarily a religion of localized spirits and personal morality, although the exact practice varies widely. Zombies are instead a by-product of the *bokor*, sorcerors who practise dark magic: they're more like hired hands who perform spells on demand, including raising the dead to act as slaves, and are quite different to voudou priests.

However, while voudou's confused reputation in the West may be courtesy of scaremongering from both European and US authorities over the centuries, it's certainly the case that the zombie finds its origins in the lands that voudou calls home. Even the word 'zombie' is derived from the Haitian-Creole *zonbi*, referring to an undead corpse revived by witchcraft.

"the GuRcH" ©2012

Islands of the Dead

Indeed, as early as the 1880s US journalist Patrick Lafcadio Hearn was describing the island of Martinique as the 'Country of the Comers-Back' (the local nickname for the island) in an essay of the same name for *Harpers* magazine. His article was an attempt to investigate local superstitions around the 'walking dead', although he was able to find little information on the subject.

However, in Haiti in 1928 another journalist, William Seabrook, encountered shuffling, glassy-eyed slave workers. He was assured they were 'zombies' – recently buried corpses apparently retrieved and reanimated by *bokor* using magical powders and spells. Local belief in zombies and fears of becoming one were so potent that the dead were often interred under heavy concrete slabs and the graves guarded to ensure peaceful – i.e. uninterrupted – decomposition.

Seabrook was prone to the sensational, but even he was dubious that these people were truly the living dead. They were, he reasoned, perhaps brain damaged or drugged. But, zombies or not, the listless, lifeless-looking slave workers were very real; what could be the cause? The work of dark magic and powders? Or perhaps people were seeing a different kind of zombie: beaten, humiliated and degraded people, deprived of their individuality and humanity and forced to work on the sugar plantations. Little wonder these 'zombies' were such mournful figures as they trudged the fields.

Bug Powder Dust

The zombie story took another twist much later, courtesy of anthropologist Wade Davis and his 1982 book *The Serpent and the Rainbow*. The Haitian zombie myth held that the dead were revived by spells and potions, then set to work; he suggested that he had found the active ingredient in the potion itself.

Not that it truly revived the dead, of course. Davis's research into the folk powders described by Seabrook and still used by *bokor* uncovered the common ingredient tetrodotoxin (TTX), derived from the venom of the puffer fish. Lethal in minute quantities when pure, he argued that a compound containing TTX would induce a death-like coma – the Haitian zombies were very much alive, but very much drugged to appear dead. Although sensational, Davis's work has never been verified or subjected to clinical trials and the scientific community remains sceptical about TTX zombification.

Nonetheless, the idea of the shuffling, mindless slave and the potent magic drug had already taken hold of Hollywood and led to the first generation of zombie movies, notably *White Zombie* (1932). Inspired by Seabrook's 1928 Haiti travelogue *The Magic Island*, it features a voodoo-enchanted heroine taken by a villainous plantation owner (called 'Murder', in case we weren't sure of his wickedness) to be a zombie slave. What a charmer.

Of course, cinema and the pop culture zombie have shuffled a long way from Haiti now – but it's important to remember the human tragedy of slavery that may lie at its roots.

'The eyes were the worst. They were in truth like the eyes of a dead man, not blind, but staring, unfocused, unseeing.... I had a sickening lapse in which I thought "maybe this stuff is really true and if it is true, it is rather awful".'

William Seabrook,
The Magic Island

Print is Dead: Zombies in Literature

Before we can talk about zombies in print, we need to take a moment to consider vampires (bear with us). Vamps are – technically at least – zombies, after all. They're living people, they get bitten (usually), they die and then come back to life as an undead creature with unnatural hunger and a penchant for getting a bit bite-y with the living. Think of them as zombie goths, if you like.

However, vampires are generally regarded as separate entities and in literature they've definitely taken a different path to zombies. Vampire fiction has a more-or-less precise moment of genesis with Polidori's short tale *The Vampyre*, written in 1819. Later, in 1897, Bram Stoker laid down the vampire rules that would be adopted throughout popular culture with *Dracula*. In the space of two novels, most of the foundations were laid.

Zombies, on the other hand, have no such fictional starting point. There's no original zombie text, and the form seems to have – appropriately – shambled into being over many years, gradually evolving into the sophisticated hyper-horror novels available today. Second cousins to their on-screen counterparts for years, the literary zombie is only now starting to come into its own.

Slow Starts

But even if there was no 'Zombies Start Here' novel, there are certainly literary ancestors of the modern zombie to investigate. Encounters between the dead and the living have been a part of humanity's stories for millennia, with some more gruesome than others.

Odysseus meets both shades of the dead in Book IX of Homer's epic poem the *Odyssey* (*c.* eighth century BC) and also the Lotus-Eaters, who have a listless, glazed appearance. Later (fourteenth century), Dante described the various miseries endured by the damned in his 'Inferno', some of which might sound familiar to Z-fans: the wrathful scratch and tear at one another; the sowers of discord are hacked to pieces but keep moving; the hypocrites shuffle aimlessly; while a grim glimpse into the ninth circle of hell reveals Count Ugolino gnawing on the head of the Archbishop Ruggieri degli Ubaldini. While not explicitly zombies, it's easy to imagine these gory visions having an impact on future writers and storytellers.

A closer example might be found a few centuries later, with the seventeenth-century *One Thousand and One Nights* (also known as *The Arabian Nights*): 'The History of Gherib and His Brother Agib' features an army of godless ghouls. (And this is classic bedtime reading, apparently.)

Be My Frankenstein

Polidori began his vampire tale on a trip to Switzerland in 1816, when he and his travelling companions were forced indoors by bad weather and took to writing stories to amuse one another. It was a creative weekend, as one of the party – Mary Shelley – came up with another hugely influential idea. She called her novel *Frankenstein*.

Brilliant but deluded, young Victor Frankenstein's meddlings with the processes of life are not detailed by Shelley (leave that to Hollywood special effects departments) so it's never clear if his first creation is a reanimated corpse or not. What's more important is the reaction it provokes: horror, fear and revulsion. Frankenstein's creature prefigures the lonely exile of zombies and examines the consequences of meddling with nature – a theme many zombie stories later return to, most notably *28 Days Later*.

Toying with the process of life and death was also on gothic supremo Edgar Allen Poe's mind when he wrote *The Facts in the Case of M. Valdemar* in 1845. Here, the narrator attempts to stave off the death of the writer Valdemar using hypnosis, succeeding only in reducing him to a catatonic state. On waking, the victim – a kind of sentient zombie – begs for death before dissolving into black slime.

Back to Life

While Poe was intrigued by life after death and the horror to be drawn from tales of being buried alive (in *The Fall of the House of Usher*, 1839, a wrongly buried woman returns from the grave seeking vengeance), his tales were not concerned with calling the dead back to life. They did, however, influence many other writers including H.P. Lovecraft, a pulp fiction writer in the 1920s.

> *'As a man with hungry teeth tears into bread, / the soul with capping head had sunk his teeth / into the other's neck, just beneath the skull (...) Lifting his mouth from this horrendous meal, / the sinner wiped off his messy lips / in the hair remaining on the chewed-up skull.'*
>
> Dante, 'Inferno'
> (from Cantos XXXII and XXXIII)

72

Lovecraft's *Herbert West – Reanimator* stories appeared in pulp magazines and blended the themes developed by Poe and – of course – Shelley in the tale of a crazed scientist who digs up and revives freshly interred corpses (the series was later turned into a comedy horror film). The dead are less than pleased to be woken: all are homicidal monsters. Again, Lovecraft doesn't specify that his undead creatures are 'zombies', but if the (rotting) shoe fits …

We've got the pulps to thank for other seedy tales of undead goings-on. They often featured stories of Haitian-like zombies, including Henry S. Whitehead's *Jumbee* (1926) and later Manly Wade Wellman's *Song of the Slaves* (1940), which features the ghoulish return from the grave of 49 African slaves murdered by a plantation owner. Alas, these are tales from a different kind of society – modern readers might be as horrified by the casual racism on display throughout the stories as they are by the events they describe.

Dead Calm

Thanks perhaps to the popularity of zombie movies, zombie fiction seems to have taken a break for a large part of the twentieth century. There are some exceptions, such as Richard Matheson's grim and chilling *I Am Legend* (1954), which almost single-handedly created the zombie apocalypse scenario and was a huge influence on Romero, but things went fairly quiet in print until the 1990s. That's when the dead … well, returned. As they do.

It began with a few anthologies such as *Book of the Dead* (1989) and *The Mammoth Book of Zombies* (1993), before writers muscled in with some full-length efforts. Brian Keene's *The Rising* (2004) introduced demonically possessed reanimated dead, while David Wellington's *Monster …* series (2004 onwards) dealt with sentient zombies bent on world domination. And it wasn't long before the Man Himself, Stephen King, turned his baleful gaze on zombies with the 2006 techno-horror of *Cell*, where mobile phones transform people into bloodthirsty undead fiends.

Moving towards the present day, the fictional zombies have picked up their pace. Max Brooks's popular series of 'factional' zombie books present a 'what if?' version of the zombie apocalypse, with *The Zombie Survival Guide* (2003) doing exactly what it says on the tin.

The Modern Way

Brooks's other zombie title is perhaps even more effective. *World War Z: An Oral History of the Zombie War* (2006) is a compelling novel told as a series of survivors' accounts of a decade-long zombie war. He presents a planet-wide event with icy plausibility, detailing how humanity might react to an extinction-level threat – through military hysteria, bureaucracy, research and acts of bravery or quiet heroism. Little surprise that the book, with its widescreen vision of zombie doom, became a Brad Pitt-fronted film in the summer of 2013.

While *World War Z* takes a serious, enquiring approach to the zombie problem, there's always room for funny zombies. And why not put them in empire-line dresses? That's what Seth Grahame-Smith has done with *Pride and Prejudice and Zombies (2009)*, a genre mashup where the undead collide with Jane Austen's heroines and heroes. Elizabeth Bennett is recast as a fearless zombie hunter, Grahame-Smith simply augmenting the Austen text with passages about the undead. It's certainly one way to breathe unlife into the classics.

From early hints of the shuffling dead to modern zomploitation tales, the zombie has now emerged as a fully-fledged literary character. There are many more zombie novels out there to explore; some challenge, some thrill, some titillate and some shock. But one thing is clear: the dead have well and truly come to take over your bookshelf. And you know how stubborn they are once they get a foothold.

'A new terror born in death, a new superstition entering the unassailable fortress of forever. I am legend.'

Seth Richard Matheson,
I am Legend

THEY WON'T STAY DEAD!
An IMAGE TEN Production
NIGHT OF THE LIVING DEAD
They keep coming back in a bloodthirsty lust for HUMAN FLESH!...
Pits the dead against the living in a struggle for survival!
Starring JUDITH O'DEA · DUANE JONES · MARILYN EASTMAN · KARL HARDMAN · JUDITH RIDLEY · KEITH WAYNE
Produced by Russel W. Streiner and Karl Hardman · Directed by George A. Romero · Screenplay by John A. Russo · A Walter Reade Organization Presentation – Released by Continental

Planet Terror: A World of Zombie Movies

While the zombie has begun to establish itself as a force in books, games and online, it's really on the big screen that the dead have been most prominent. Both before and after Romero's *Night of the Living Dead* there were many zombie flicks of varying quality, some deserving their cult status and some equally deserving a mouldering fate in some forgotten basement.

Zombie films come in many forms, and not all of them horrifying. Zombies can thrill and chill, of course, but they've also become amusing, intriguing and – more recently – even romantic. It's just another reason why they're such versatile creations.

Early Zombie Films

The very first zombie films in the 1930s and 1940s were heavily influenced by the idea of the Haitian zombie, a slave returned from the dead by sinister witchcraft. We've mentioned *White Zombie* already, but there were many others, with ever-more weird and wonderful titles: witness the dubious delights of *Revolt of the Zombies* (1936) or *The Corpse Vanishes* (1942), all playing on similar themes with varying degrees of success. *I Walked With A Zombie* (1943) is a more subtle affair that's more melodrama than horror, but it stands alone with its restraint and thoughtful appraisal of Haitian voodoo.

Co.

'It gets up and kills! The people it kills get up and kill!'

Dr. Foster,
Dawn of the Dead, 1978

'Fine? We just killed our girlfriend with a chainsaw. Does that sound "fine"?'

Ash, Evil Dead 2

As the 1950s progressed, the world moved away from voodoo and was lured by the promise of jet packs and science fiction, so the zombies attempted to move with the times (always tricky when you're a living corpse), but with limited success. Atomic paranoia consumed the world and posed a far more realistic world-ending threat to audiences, so what hope did zombies have? With the exception of *Invasion of the Body Snatchers* (1956 and again in 1978), it was not a fun decade for the undead.

Things looked up in the Swinging Sixties, however, with Hammer's 1966 *Plague of the Zombies* embracing the sorcery theme and the first adaptation of Matheson's novel *I Am Legend*, *The Last Man on Earth* (1964, starring Vincent Price), striking a grim post-apocalyptic note.

The World After the Night Before

Everything then changed with the release of *The Night of the Living Dead* in 1968, with Romero effectively rebooting the entire idea of the zombie. Directors from all over the world were quick to hop onto the new zombie bandwagon in the 1960s and 70s, leading to some curious Italian efforts – who's for zombie knights, folks? – in films such as *Tombs of the Blind Dead* in 1971.

'Before we get through with this thing we may uncover sins that even the devil would be ashamed of.'

Dr Bruner,
White Zombie, 1932

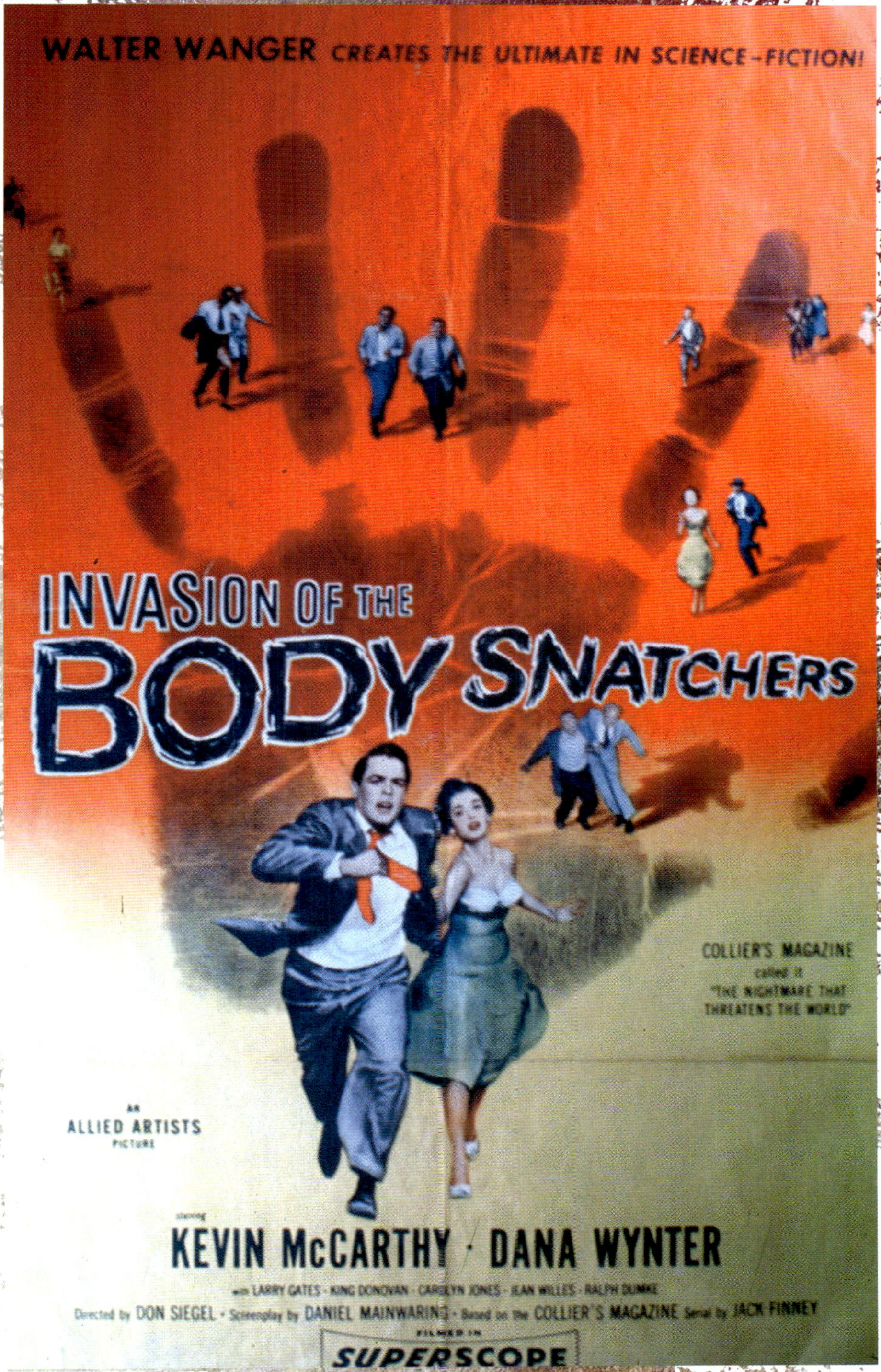
WALTER WANGER CREATES THE ULTIMATE IN SCIENCE-FICTION!
INVASION OF THE
BODY SNATCHERS
COLLIER'S MAGAZINE
called it
"THE NIGHTMARE THAT
THREATENS THE WORLD"
AN
ALLIED ARTISTS
PICTURE
KEVIN McCARTHY · DANA WYNTER
Directed by DON SIEGEL · Screenplay by DANIEL MAINWARING · Based on the COLLIER'S MAGAZINE Serial by JACK FINNEY
SUPERSCOPE

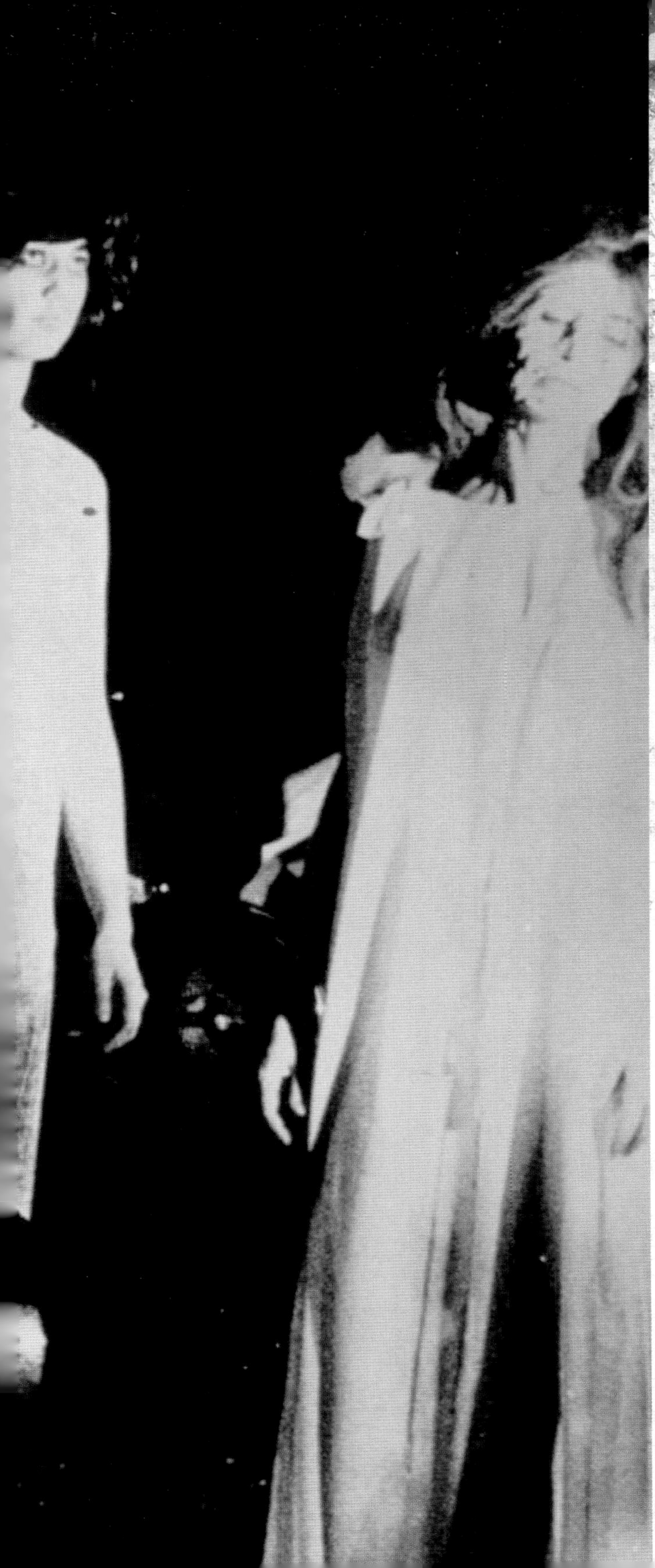

'I go to conventions and universities and talk to young filmmakers and everybody's making a zombie movie! It's because it's easy to get the neighbours to come out, put some ketchup on them.'

George A. Romero

The rotting flesh of the zombies in these films was only rivalled by the exposed flesh of the various nubile young women at their mercy as zombie flicks became more titillating, culminating in Lucio Fulci's audacious *Zombie* (or *Zombie Flesh Eaters*) in 1978. Exploiting a loophole that allowed him to promote his film as *Zombi 2* in the original theatrical release and therefore falsely positioning it as a sequel to *Dawn of the Dead* (1978), it ticks all the apocalypse boxes: splattering blood and gore, a mysterious island, the dead bursting from the ground and a final-frame shock of the zombies wandering across Brooklyn Bridge. And a topless scuba diving woman witnessing an underwater zombie vs shark battle, of course.

Unsurprisingly, the film proved influential and, as the 1980s wore on, the outfits grew skimpier and the gore more outrageous. The quality, on the other hand....

King of Comedy

While Europe plumbed the depths with ever more pornographic carve ups like *Zombie Holocaust*, the US turned to slasher movies such as the 1980 *Friday the 13th* (Jason is to all intents and purposes an unkillable zombie) and established the 'horny teens get laid and slayed' trope that still runs throughout horror cinema today.

NORMAN WARD.

L
SECOND ISSUE COLLECTORS' EDITION!
15¢
CREEPSHOW 2
JOLTING TALES OF HORROR!
FORTUNE
MARTIN
LIFE
THE STAND
DAWN OF THE DEAD
CREEPSHOW
SMALL WORLD
TIME
FIRE-STARTER
NEW WORLD PICTURES presents A LAUREL PRODUCTION CREEPSHOW II
written by GEORGE ROMERO produced by DAVID BALL executive producer RICHARD RUBINSTEIN directed by MICHAEL GORNICK
NEW WORLD PICTURES
BILLING NOT CONTRACTUAL
©1986 NEW WORLD PICTURES. ALL RIGHTS RESERVED.

'You know, I don't think I've got it in me to shoot my flatmate, my mum, and my girlfriend all in the same night.'

Shaun, Shaun of the Dead

With the possible exception of Romero and Stephen King's horror anthology movie *Creepshow* (1982) it was all getting pretty nasty, so a little light relief was welcome when Sam Raimi's cast found themselves in a cabin in the woods. The *Evil Dead* trilogy (from 1981) made a cult hero of actor Bruce Campbell and walked an entertaining line between farce and fear as Campbell's character Ash chops, shoots, chainsaws, stumbles and screams his way through various traumas that would snap a lesser man's sanity like a twig.

Speaking of twigs, lest it get too scary, the *Dead* … films also include groping trees. And flying eyeballs. The occasional dancing zombie, too. Raimi flings everything at his hero and delivers genuine shocks alongside genuine comedy, the films becoming increasingly comedic as they go along. There's nothing like watching an undead ghoul literally *burst* and shower the good guys in green goop to pick you up after a hard day, right?

Twenty-First Century Breakdown

Whether scary or comedic (let's hear it for the 1985 *Return of the Living Dead*!), 1980s and '90s zombie flicks were generally all about the group jeopardy and a one-off uprising of evil. Post millennium (and perhaps post 9/11) though, the scale increased and the return of the zombie apocalypse brought global jeopardy films back into the frame.

These movies included the ever-expanding *Resident Evil* (2002) franchise and new instalments of Romero's vision with *Land of the Dead* (2005), as well as a *Dawn of the Dead* (2004) remake that angered and delighted horror fans in equal measure, and the Tarantino/Rodriguez B-movie treat *Planet Terror*. But with the end of times came the beginning of a new wave of zombie movies that really thrust the undead into the big time.

First up, low-budget Danny Boyle shocker *28 Days Later* (2002) brought the fear back and controversially introduced the 'running zombie' – not really undead, but infected with Rage, a virus that turns people into sprinting, blood-vomiting, terrifying homicidal maniacs. Purists tutted and Edgar Wright's *Shaun of the Dead* determinedly slowed the Zs down again in 2004, with Simon Pegg and Nick Frost retreating to the pub to face the end of the world. Combining slapstick, genuine horror and witty social commentary alongside its planet-wide calamity, *Shaun* is both an affectionate nod to Romero and a genre-re-invigorating shot in the arm.

'Guys struggle talking to girls in the best of times. So add on the fact that you're undead, you're rotting away and you can't really talk at all, and she's terrified of you, it makes it very tricky.'

Nicholas Hoult on Warm Bodies

Love You to Death

Bringing things towards the present day, *Zombieland* (2009) takes the best bits of horror, road movies and zombie apocalypse conventions, to offer up a refreshingly upbeat take on the genre. Dropping in survival rules with a knowing wink (such as remembering to always shoot zombies in the head twice), plus a deft measure of pleasing romance and an inspired Bill Murray cameo, it succeeds on every level. Even more genre-defying, *Warm Bodies* (2013), based on Isaac Marion's novel, explores a human/zombie love affair in a cute way that's definitely not as gross as it sounds.

Which brings us up to date with zombies in the hands of Brad Pitt (wait! Come back!). *World War Z* does a good job of conveying the scale of a planet-wide zombie pandemic, although those pesky running zombies show up again (ignoring the shambling Zs of the original novel) and some were left frustrated by the lack of gore. However, Pitt is an ever-watchable screen presence and the film maintained a decent level of tension (and performed well at the box office), so there's talk of sequels in the next few years; time will tell.

Whatever happens to Pitt vs Zack though, the recent crop of high-quality zombie films show that the undead are in rude health at the multiplex: it's likely that the dead will continue to have their day at the movies for a good while yet. Now, what's that groaning noise from the projection booth?

'Her dirty blonde hair hung in patches from her tight, leathery skin. I centered my sight between her shrunken, milky blue eyes.... The round knocked her on her back, steam coming from the hole in her forehead.'

Max Brooks, World War Z

Wherefore Art Thou, Romero? Zombie Cinema's Shakespeare

The world was not a serene place in 1968. Riots raged on the streets of London, Paris and Chicago while the US sank further into the mire of the Vietnam war. Robert Kennedy was assassinated, while heavy-handed police action at a civil rights march in Northern Ireland contributed to the start of 'The Troubles'. Astronauts on Apollo 8 became the first men to see the dark side of the moon even as *2001: A Space Odyssey* appeared in cinemas. Add to this the return of Elvis in *that* white suit, and it made for a tumultuous year.

Hardly surprising then that on its initial release George A. Romero's *Night of the Living Dead* didn't create too many ripples. But as the reviews started to come in, dubbing it an 'unrelieved orgy of sadism' (thanks, *Variety*), it quickly began to churn up tidal waves that would eventually swamp all of horror cinema. The movie grossed $12 million in the US ($33 million globally), put Pennsylvania on the map as the capital of zombie cinema, totally and irreducibly redefined the concept of the zombie and elevated writer/director Romero to legendary status amongst a legion of fans.

All Right on the Night

Actually, 'legend' is an appropriate term when considering *Night of the Living Dead*, as Romero has often cited novelist Richard Matheson's dystopian bleak-fest *I Am Legend* as one

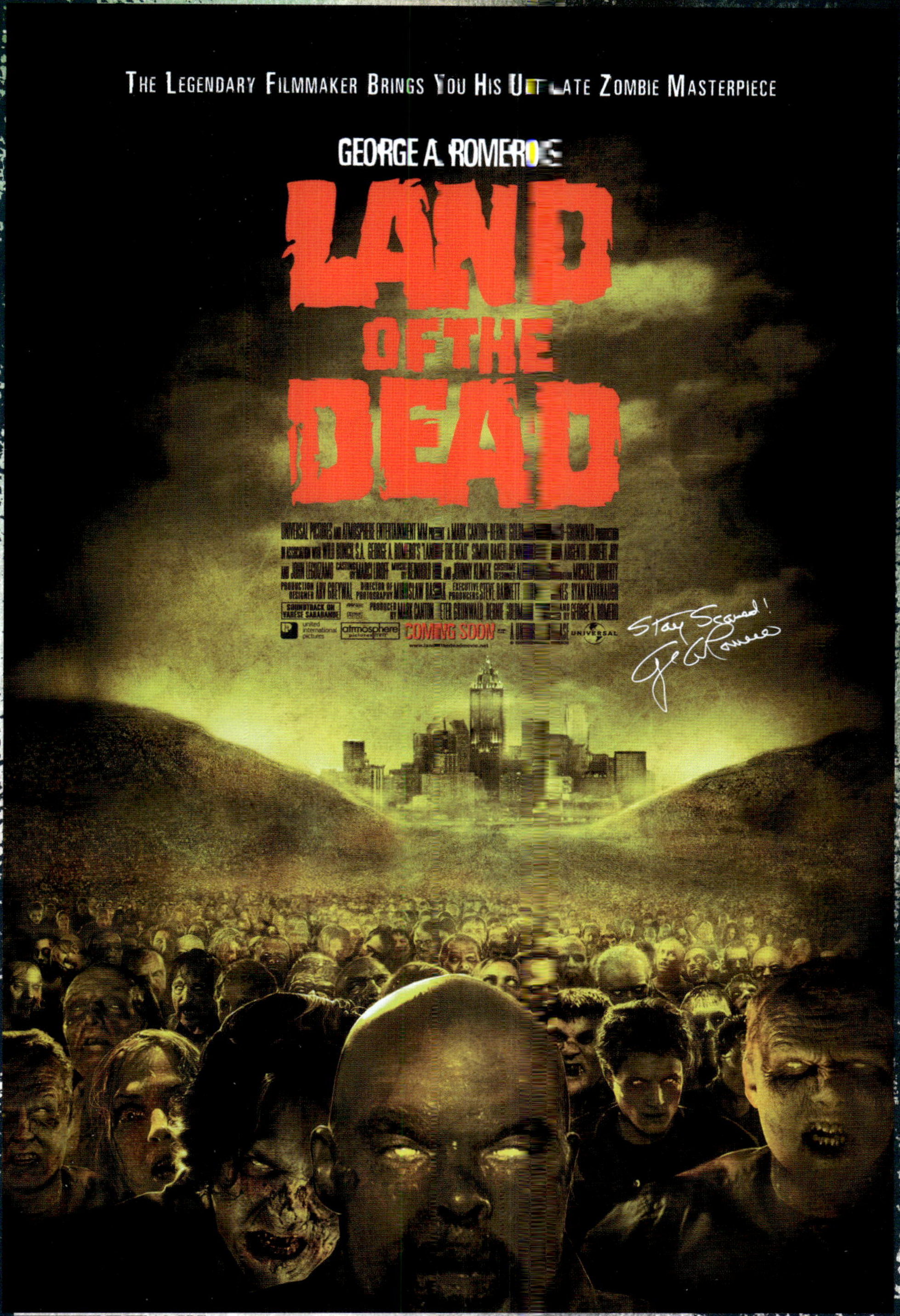
THE LEGENDARY FILMMAKER BRINGS YOU HIS ULTIMATE ZOMBIE MASTERPIECE
GEORGE A. ROMERO'S
LAND OF THE DEAD
COMING SOON
Stay Scared!

of the principal sources of inspiration for his script (the unsettled world outside surely contributed, too). There are clear similarities: both centre on a hunted survivor (or survivors) terrorized by undead creatures, hiding out in a shuttered-up house and trying desperately to survive.

Night … is unique for many reasons, but perhaps its best trick is being rated as the most important zombie movie ever made without actually ever referring to zombies. Romero's creatures are reanimated corpses, yes, but are dubbed 'ghouls' throughout proceedings; we never learn their true origin, but it's hinted via newscasts (at the insistence of the film's producers, apparently) that radiation from a returned space probe is the cause. There's that space age paranoia again, moving the zombie firmly away from the supernatural.

Of course this is merely a semantic curiosity, as the undead creatures that the beleaguered souls in Romero's cabin are battling are definitely zombies. However, at this point Romero hadn't nailed down all the rules that would become so important to his later films (and everyone else's). His zombies walk and moan, yes, but they seem very fresh, exhibit some evidence of strategic thought and even pick up clubs.

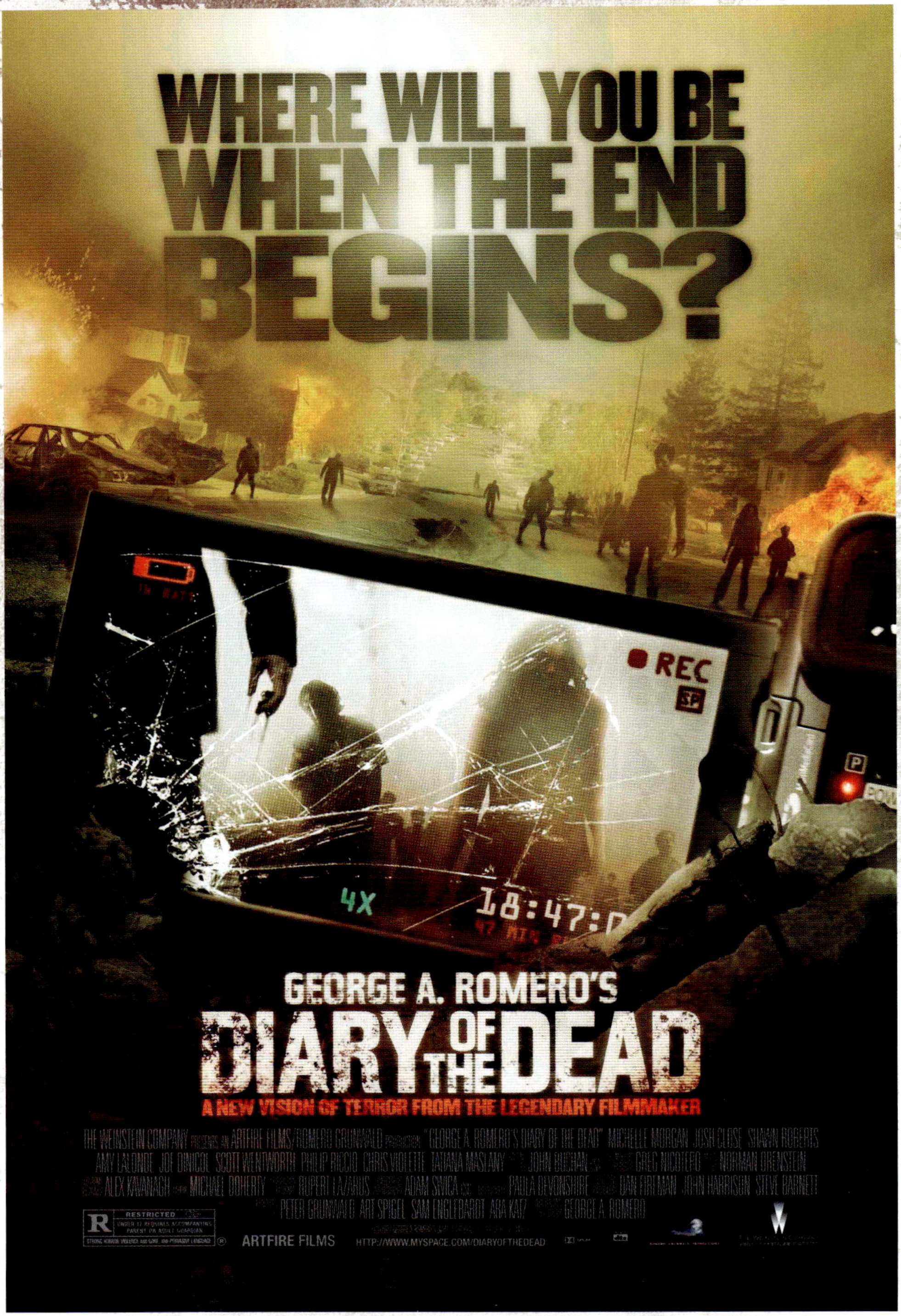
WHERE WILL YOU BE
WHEN THE END
BEGINS?
REC
SP
4X
18:47:0
GEORGE A. ROMERO'S
DIARY OF THE DEAD
A NEW VISION OF TERROR FROM THE LEGENDARY FILMMAKER
THE WEINSTEIN COMPANY PRESENTS AN ARTFIRE FILMS/ROMERO GRUNWALD PRODUCTION "GEORGE A. ROMERO'S DIARY OF THE DEAD" MICHELLE MORGAN JOSH CLOSE SHAWN ROBERTS
AMY LALONDE JOE DINICOL SCOTT WENTWORTH PHILIP RICCIO CHRIS VIOLETTE TATIANA MASLANY JOHN BUCHAN GREG NICOTERO NORMAN ORENSTEIN
ALEX KAVANAGH MICHAEL DOHERTY RUPERT LAZARUS ADAM SWICA PAULA DEVONSHIRE DAN FIREMAN JOHN HARRISON STEVE BARNETT
PETER GRUNWALD ART SPIGEL SAM ENGLEBARDT ARA KATZ GEORGE A. ROMERO
R RESTRICTED
UNDER 17 REQUIRES ACCOMPANYING PARENT OR ADULT GUARDIAN
ARTFIRE FILMS
HTTP://WWW.MYSPACE.COM/DIARYOFTHEDEAD

'They're dead. They're all messed up.'

Chief McLelland, *Night of the Living Dead*

'Something Granddad used to tell us: when there's no more room in hell, the dead will walk the Earth.'

Peter, *Dawn of the Dead*

Bad to the Bone

One thing that's definitely established, though, is the zombies' lust for human flesh. After *Night* … all zombies would be after a human snack. Even now, the feeding scenes in the movie, complete with tearing strips of flesh and gooey entrails, are shocking viewing.

Romero's reinvention of the zombie – and zombie movie – stretched to other areas, too. His characters are horribly flawed and effectively engineer their own deaths through in-fighting and inept decision-making. He also introduced the nihilistic tone and global apocalypse conceit that have become zombie standards.

After the success of *Night of the Living Dead*, fans had to wait until 1978 for *Dawn of the Dead*, which was made in the grand tradition of sequels: everything bigger and badder. More zombies and astonishing levels of brain-bursting gore – plus the trademark Romero swipes at capitalism, consumerism (and any other 'ism' you care to mention). This time there's no cause for the zombie plague – they just show up, and we're dropped right into the middle of a planet-wide crisis following a small group (again) as they make for the mall. A few more zombie rules are introduced here – their bites are fatal, for example, and however slow (or far away) Z is, any character who looks down to reload their gun will be instantly surrounded and munched.

Dead and Dead Again

By the third instalment, *Day of the Dead*, the zombies are doing so well that mankind is locked in a bunker, bickering over what to do next. The film somehow manages to ratchet the violence up even further: faces are torn off, uneaten food is ripped from eviscerated torsos ... and we even get Bub, a pet zombie (later echoed in both *28 Days Later* and *Shaun of the Dead*). The fourth film, *Land of the Dead*, increased the scale, although more recent Romero works such as *Diary of the Dead* (2007) have dialled things down again.

Romero's films, though visionary, are far from perfect. There's surely no excuse for the absurd blue-skinned zombies of *Dawn of the Dead*, and his dialogue often seems to have been written by someone who's never had a conversation with a real person, ever (an ailment George Lucas later suffered from with *Star Wars*).

However, there's also no escaping their brilliance. The style, imagination and sheer audacity of *Night of the Living Dead* alone gave zombies a new lease of death, basically erasing everything that had gone before and starting again from scratch. If you're new to contemporary zombie cinema, Romero's films are the place to start: everything we know about Z, we learned from him. He truly is the king of the dead.

RKDALE
SPITA

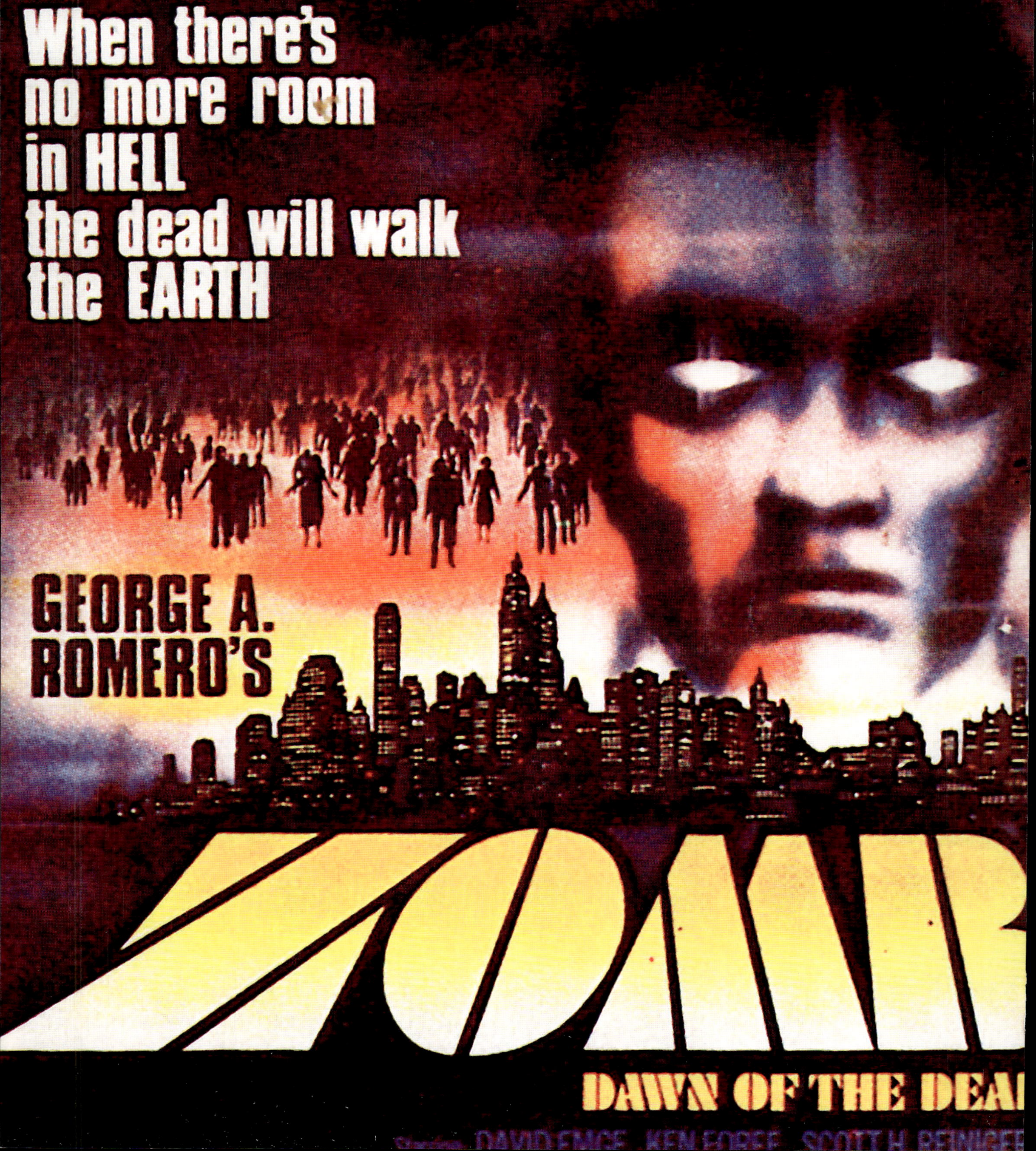
When there's
no more room
in HELL
the dead will walk
the EARTH
GEORGE A.
ROMERO'S
DAWN OF THE DEA

'I always thought of the zombies as being about revolution, one generation consuming the next.'

George A. Romero

Sears Tower

Undead Visions: Zombies in Art

You might expect any self-respecting zombie with even a trace of vanity left to be a camera-shy creature, eschewing the limelight. But zombies throughout the ages have been terrible posers, featuring in many different kinds of art

It's easy to see why they're appealing subjects for artists. These are creatures at once real and unreal, offering a rare challenge to present life and death in one image. What expression does a walking corpse have? How do you deal with the eyes? And then, of course, there's all that ragged flesh and general oozing to contend with.

Early Images

As the idea of the undead has been with us for a long while, it follows that images of the walking dead would also crop up regularly throughout the history of art. And so it proves: early pictorial representations of the dead (or the souls of the dead) can even be found in the *Egyptian Book of the Dead* (1550–50 BC).

Perhaps one of the more memorable medieval pieces featuring the dead is *The Dead Lovers* (around 1470, artist unknown), an arresting and macabre image featuring a naked man and woman who might not look out of place on a zombie walk. Their skin is sallow and sunken, their flesh riven with wounds and plucked at by animals and insects, lips drawn back into grisly leers. There's a terrible beauty to the portrait, especially the snakes bursting in and out of their bodies (yes, really), as it becomes clear that these corpses are very much animate beings, one touching the other tenderly on the shoulder.

Meanwhile, for an even darker vision of the dead, Gustav Doré's illustrations of both Dante's 'Inferno' and Coleridge's 'Rime of the Ancient Mariner' in the nineteenth century provide suitable shadow.

Dark Doré

Doré's hell-bound souls in 'Inferno' are tormented for sure, but more chilling is his rendering of Coleridge's 'Night-mare Life-in-Death', a pale undead woman who plays dice with the incarnation of Death for the souls of the crew in 'Rime of the Ancient Mariner'. In Doré's engraving she leans forward over the dice with dark-eyed intensity, her skin mottled and hair blowing around her, as the hooded figure of Death looks on impassively. More than a century on, the image retains the power to raise goosebumps – as does a panel from later in the tale as the dead crew reanimate, sunken eyed (and presumably moaning) to steer the stricken ship.

'To me, the best zombie movies aren't the splatter fests of gore and violence with goofy characters and tongue in cheek antics. Good zombie movies show us how messed up we are, they make us question our station in society... and our society's station in the world.'

Robert Kirkman

Squirm of the Century

The advent of pulp magazines in the late nineteenth and early twentieth centuries provided many memorable opportunities for zombie tales, and of course illustrations to accompany them – titles such as *Weird Tales*, *Strange Tales* and *Ghost Stories* ran zombie-like offerings in the 1920s and 1930s with curious cover and interior art to match.

Around the same time, Harry Clarke's illustrations of Edgar Allen Poe's tales were also striking some gothic poses. His image for *The Facts in the Case of M. Valdemar* in particular practically drips with unctuous, putrescent gore (and not in a good way). Jaw-dropping for rather less edifying reasons, the artistic merit of Alexander King's drawings for W.B. Seabrook's early zombie book *The Magic Island* is overshadowed by the racist caricaturing of the black slaves he depicts as zombies.

Later in the century, things really took off for zombie art on the newsstands with a surge of horror comics. Titles of the 1950s, such as the *Vault of Horror* and *Tales from the Crypt*, boasted lurid art from the likes of Johnny Craig and Jack Davis, complete with axes buried in undead heads or still-juicy zombies rising from the grave.

The Comic Dead

Needless to say, the upfront gore of these titles quickly fell foul of the new Comics Code in 1954, but zombies – as you might expect – just kept coming back. Resurrected in magazine format in titles such as *Creepy* and *Eerie*, with art from fantasy master Frank Frazetta among others, the dead walked again in lurid oil colours.

Heading into the last decades of the century, things got even more graphic, courtesy of titles such as the short-lived *Twisted Tales* in 1982 – the debut issue featured a story illustrated by Alfredo Alcala in which a vengeful zombie rises from a watery grave. A comic book adaptation of Raimi treat *Army of Darkness* followed in 1992, paving the way for the smash zombie hits that were to follow.

Perhaps the best known of these (courtesy of the current TV adaptation) is *The Walking Dead*, Robert Kirkman's no-nonsense account of a post-zombie-apocalypse world. With work from artists including Tony Moore and Charlie Adlard, it's an evocative piece that nicely captures the human tensions and corporeal horror of a worldwide catastrophe.

Not to be outdone by his earlier creation, Kirkman and Marvel comics hit on the bright idea of making their iconic heroes a little bit more, well, dead. Cue zombie Spiderman, Captain America and Hulk in *Marvel Zombies*. Yes, that's right. You can probably imagine the undead treats within – Zombie Hulk does indeed smash.

'You know that when we die, we become them. You think we hide behind walls to protect us from the walking dead? Don't you get it? We ARE the walking dead!'

Robert Kirkman,
The Walking Dead

More Zom Coms

Other comics have also embraced the zombie, whether it's quirky indies like IGN's *Zombies vs Robots* or encounters between iconic characters. In the peerless Batman story *The Long Halloween*, for example, the Dark Knight meets Solomon Grundy, a kind of super-zombie (and the first to appear in comics, in 1944), in the sewers beneath Gotham. Grundy is locked in a constant cycle of death and rebirth, a towering, gigantic undead being brought powerfully to life by Jeph Loeb and Tim Sale. Rather more pared back, Norwegian artist Jason's comic *The Living and the Dead* is another low-key masterpiece – it's a simply drawn black-and-white zombie romance, and the world can always use more of those.

Modern Macabre

Away from the panels of comic books, the zombie is in rude health in other areas of art. Concept art for movies and games is a rich hunting ground for zed heads, for instance: Atomhawk's work for the *Dead Island Riptide* game seems to reference the Hudson Bay zombies in Fulci's *Zombie Flesh Eaters* but adds all the modern sheen we've come to expect, complete with contusions and rent flesh in marvellous 3D.

Similarly, Joe Roberts (pages 95 and 104) relied on the horror standard 'hand blasting out from the grave' for his cover art for a Nintendo magazine – with the added twist of the undead hand clasping a Wii remote. Modern zombie art is a fusion of traditional shock and gore with playful new elements, keeping that tongue in cheek approach so beloved of directors like Raimi and Jackson.

'I keep a little notebook of things that I can do to the zombies that might be silly and fun.'

George A. Romero

It's worth remembering as well that zombie movies have boasted some fine poster art over the years, whether it's the real eyes in a dead skull of *Evil Dead*, the over-the-top gorefest nonsense of Jerry Gross's *I Drink Your Blood* and *I Eat Your Skin* or the punkish album cover look to *The Return of the Living Dead* (page 89). And for a fresh spin on a classic, Olly Moss's reworking of *The Evil Dead* is a clean, beautifully-executed poster that's both reverential homage and crisp new concept.

Dead Good Art

Of course, just as zombies have proven they can hold their own as the central draw of a movie or game for years now (well you don't go to see the carefully characterized, soon-to-be-lunch zombie fodder, do you?), so they can also be the subject of fantasy and horror art in their own right.

Modern zombie art comes in a range of shapes and sizes and might be created (brought back to life?) in any medium. While digital tools such as Corel and Photoshop are increasingly popular, some artists still prefer to get their hands dirty with oils, watercolours, pencils … even tattoo machines. As any outbreak survivor will tell you, that's the thing with zombies: you need to improvize and be adaptable.

'Someone in this village is practising witchcraft. That corpse wandering on the moors is an undead, a zombie.'

Sir James Forbes,
The Plague of the Zombies, 1966

Digi-zombies may crawl from the wires with theatrical blur and light, as seen in Alexandrescu Paul's work (page 70); or they may adopt an Old Master painterly feel. Alan Lathwell's undead creations (page 75), for example, make use of oil-like techniques with a sombre result. His pieces are elegiac renderings of the undead, much more introspective than the high-octane bloodbaths of other zombie incarnations.

Speaking of which … for a battle-drenched take on the undead, some digital artists prefer to reference the classic 1960s era of sword and sorcery art, complete with bulging biceps and much mayhem; Mike Penn in particular does a great job in this arena (page 103).

They Live!

On the traditional side, there are as many approaches to illustrating zombies as there are ingenious ways to drop them in the movies (lawnmower, anyone?). Jon Procter keeps it strong and simple with scratchy, hectic black and white linework, for example, while Dino Tomic (page 69) represents the pencillers out there – his pieces embrace realism in a big way, creating zombies that look about ready to pop out of the page.

'They're coming to get you, Barbra!'

Johnny,
Night of the Living Dead, 1968

'Send… More… Paramedics…'

Zombie, The Return of the Living Dead, 1985

THE
RETURN
OF THE
LIVING
DEAD

"the GURCH" ©200

'Zombies are the middle children of the otherworldly family. Vampires are the oldest brother who gets to have a room in the attic, all tripped out with a disco ball and shag carpet. Werewolves are the youngest, the babies, always getting pinched and told they're cute. With all that attention stolen away from the middle child Zombie, no wonder she shuffles off grumbling, "Marsha, Marsha, Marsha".'

Kevin James Breaux

For something more impressionistic in the vein of classic Frazetta or Vallejo, The Gurch (pages 15, 78, 82) is the go-to guy with his ragged oil and watercolour zombies that seem to drip and pant on the page. Or if you want something even more visceral, you can't beat tattoo art: we're talking actual blood and skin getting involved here, after all. The acknowledged horror master is New Yorker Paul Booth, whose realistic tattoos proudly wear the influence of surrealist H.R. Geiger as well as a host of scary movies and Booth's own unique mind. Zombies pop up everywhere in tattoo art – it's common to see zombie Marilyns, zombie pin-ups, zombies peeping out from behind trompe l'oeil torn flesh ... you name it.

In fact, the pervasive influence of zombies on tattoo art shows just how far they have worked their way into the cultural consciousness. From early proto-zombie drawings, engravings and paintings to movie poster art and pulp magazines, right through to getting zombies inked onto us permanently, our attitude to zombies in art shows that they have – in every sense – really managed to get under our skin.

Playtime's Over: Zombies & Video Games

Picture the scene. Disturbing reports of grisly goings-on are coming in. Your special forces colleagues are sent out to investigate, but they never come back. So in you go, with the members of Alpha team, to find out what happened. You find their helicopter abandoned, no trace of your comrades, and a pack of murderous dogs keen to turn you into dinner. What to do? It seems like a good idea to hide out in that mansion over there until things calm down. Surely nothing can get you in there? After all, what's the worst that could happen?

Evil in the House

That's the set-up for 1996's *Resident Evil*, one of the most successful zombie video games of recent years, if not ever. Players entered the house in Raccoon City to find that the worse that could happen was a house inhabited by decidedly unfriendly undead fiends, ready for mayhem. The game is an early example of 'survival horror', pitting players against legions of mutated people, animals and plants, all turned into zombies by the pernicious T-virus.

The game played as a third-person shooter and clearly came steeped in zombie lore and gore. Victims trapped in a spooky house? Check. Shuffling zombies? Check. Blood and scares?

AMONKS

'I expect a zombie to show up on Sesame Street soon, teaching kids to count.'

George A. Romero

in abundance. *Resident Evil* ushered in a new era of genuinely creepy gameplay that provided the thrills and spills of a classic shoot-em-up with a new level of challenges and strategy, all of which combined to make it an instant hit.

The formula clearly worked, as there have been many successive sequels and spin-offs to the original game – at time of writing the game is up to its sixth iteration, with different versions taking players further afield into the troubled Raccoon City to face off against zombies of all kinds; including the chainsaw-wielding variety.

Game On

Zombies could have been made for video games. Who wouldn't want the thrill and challenge of facing their nightmares and taking on the undead hordes? So, although *Resident Evil* took both the zombie theme and survival horror genre to new levels, it certainly wasn't the first zombie game. Previous incarnations had included a 1980s blocky *Evil Dead* game, the puzzler *Alone in the Dark* and even a zombie pirate starring in the second *Monkey Island* adventure from Ubisoft. There's probably a zombie argument to be made for 1993's daftly violent *Doom*, as well as although the creatures taken to task with fists, shotguns, chainsaws and plasma rifles were 'demons', there was more than a trace of the Romero walking dead in them.

And of course, many, many games followed *Resident Evil*, although few even approached its success (however well they played as games). *House of the Dead* eschewed puzzle-solving niceties in favour of axe-flinging zombies to create a

series of on-rails arcade shooters, complete with hulking end of level bosses and annoying ninja undead. Yes, ninja undead.

Other memorable titles included Capcom's *Dead Rising*, which pitted a band of plucky survivors in a shopping mall against undead hordes. Sound familiar? The game did allow you to beat zombies to death with cones and shopping trolleys, which certainly mixed things up a little, as did the cooperative play introduced by Valve's *Left 4 Dead*, which also included bile-spitting infected creatures. Nice.

Another Turn

Like the undead themselves, zombie games have proved to be somewhat unstoppable, and the release of a new game – 2013's *The Last of Us* – is no exception. Following an apocalypse-level infection event, mankind is reduced to fungus-faced zombies and the few survivors battle for existence amongst the rotting concrete jungles of civilization. The game features new levels of sophistication in gameplay, AI, combat and – perhaps most vitally – story, and has reinvigorated the genre, gaining top-level reviews and general acclaim along the way.

As computers and consoles have evolved, many characters have come and gone, but it looks like the grim steps of the undead will be haunting our gaming sessions for a long while yet. There is, after all, a darkly satisfying feeling to blasting a zombie to bits, and that will never go away.

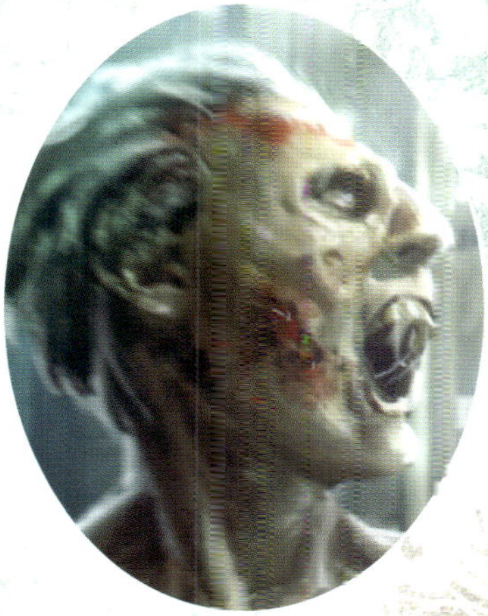

From the Grave to your Living Room: Zombies on TV

No self-respecting zombie apocalypse could be complete without the undead making their way into our front rooms and onto our TV screens, and that's exactly what they've been doing over the past few decades. With gradually increasing regularity, zombies have escaped from the movies, or the pages of comics and novels, and have become stars of the small screen as well. They might appear in their own shows, as bit-parts in more established series, as one-off scares … or they might go one further and help create the most successful and culturally significant music video of all time. But more of that in a moment.

Early Cameos

For a cult TV programme that languished in relative obscurity until fairly recently, the US gothic soap *Dark Shadows* (1966–71) managed to break new ground in a few important ways. It did something to the mind of a young Johnny Depp, for one thing, for which twenty-first century cinema should probably be grateful – the actor was a fan of the original series (and starred in the 2012 remake), which presumably helped foster his predilection for the odd and the offbeat.

The show also featured one of the first sympathetic vampire characters, pre-dating *Twilight* and its ilk by many decades, with the creation of Barnabas Collins. But not content with that, one storyline had an undead twist – Quentin Collins becomes a zombie, to the consternation of the family, complete with mandatory moaning and roaming. However, there's a happy ending: his zombism seems to be caused by a curse (much like early zombie legends) and is reversed, restoring him to life in the end.

No such luck for the reanimated dead who rose to plague the cast of *Buffy the Vampire Slayer* in the 1990s. Summoned by a spooky African mask in the 'Dead Man's Party' episode, the recently dead gatecrash a party and generally put a damper on the fun and frolics.

Darker Shadows

In keeping with the ever-darker tone of the show, zombies returned to *Buffy …* in horrific style at the close of the later episode 'Forever'. A desperate Dawn attempts to use magic to recall her dead mother from the grave – we see a chilling shot of bare feet stumbling through the grass and hear a heavy knock on the door before the spell is mercifully broken and the creature vanishes.

Various other shows (including *Buffy* spin-off *Angel*) have flirted with zombies, and there have been made-for-TV specials that have used them to good effect. The UK's *Dead Set*, written by none-more-dark journalist and critic Charlie Brooker, was a smart 2005 short series imagining the cast of a *Big Brother*-style reality show holed up in their TV cage while a zombie apocalypse goes on outside. In the end it gets in – but the question is, who is more horrifying: the brain hungry zombies, or the fame hungry contestants? You decide.

'Grisly ghouls from every tomb are closing in to seal your doom.'

Vincent Price, voiceover in Michael Jackson's 'Thriller'

'Hey you. Dumbass. Yeah, you in the tank. Cosy in there?'

Glenn, The Walking Dead

Zombies made appearances in US serials *Masters of Horror* and *Fear Itself*, while in the UK the required behind-the-sofa viewing came courtesy of – who else? – *Doctor Who*. Various undead critters have plagued the Doctor, from the corpses of 'The Unquiet Dead' (battled with help from Charles Dickens) to the gas-mask faced revenants of 'The Empty Child'.

The Midnight Hour is Close at Hand

Back to that music video, then. If any zombie ever made an impression on the living rooms of the world, it was the zombie incarnation of Michael Jackson in the singer's 1983 video for the song 'Thriller' (from the album of the same name). Clocking in at a hefty 14 minutes long and with guest voiceover from horror legend Vincent Price, it's often regarded as the greatest music video ever made and its iconic dance has spawned many imitations on dancefloors all over the planet.

'Thriller's' statistics are intimidating. The number of views are estimated to be into the billions (it's currently garnered 20 million Facebook 'likes' on Jackson's official website), with sales running to tens of millions. It's also been inducted into the National Film Registry by the Library of Congress in the US, the first music video to do so, for being 'culturally, historically or aesthetically significant. If the aliens land, we'll be showing them 'Thriller'.

Shot by *An American Werewolf in London* director John Landis (who also wrote the story with Jackson), the story needs no explanation here – doubtless you're one of the viewing billions – but suffice it to say it introduced the grooving zombie, some truly killer dance moves and a glorious signature cackle from Price (who cameos in the final frame of the video). Even thirty years on, it still thrills.

Walking Blues

Coming more up to date, BBC series *In the Flesh* takes a novel approach to zombies – or rather, those suffering from 'Partially Deceased Syndrome'. How would we help them fit back into society, rather than resorting to the old shotgun/head routine? Perhaps even more engaging is the question of what the zombies themselves would make of their predicament and how they'd confront families of people they killed. How do you reconcile yourself with the neighbours when you ate one of them? Bit awkward.

Across the pond, the current AMC series *The Walking Dead* couldn't be much more removed from the tongue in cheek theatrical scares of 'Thriller' or Anglo-quirkiness of *In the Flesh* (and if it's quirkiness you're after, check out the deliciously macabre *The Returned*, also from the UK, for a more supernatural take on the undead). Based on the graphic novel by Robert Kirkman, Tony Moore and Charlie Adlard, the Frank Darabont-helmed show opens in the hissing heat of a brutal summer and quickly ushers in the horror as a lone police officer confronts a girl in an abandoned petrol station. She turns to reveal a rotten, grinning leer and he shoots her in the head, terrified. It's a bold beginning and the series has yet to ease off the pace, pitting survivors of a catastrophic global pandemic against both zombies and each other.

At the time of writing, the dead are still very much walking, showing that – as with so many things – zombies have found their way into every aspect of our lives, and they're not going anywhere. Well, not fast, anyway.

'Unbelievable. "Do you like my mask? Isn't it pretty? It raises the dead!" Americans.'

Giles, Buffy the Vampire Slayer: Dead Man's Party

'In the head. You've got to get them in the head.'

Kelly, Dead Set

Dead Addictive: Even More Sources of Zombie Fun

It's unlikely, but if you should find that you've worked your way through every zombie movie (and every vaguely related movie), read the novels, pored over the comics, and watched box sets until your eyes resemble an extra from *28 Days Later*, there's no need to panic. There are many other ways to get a zombie fix. Some of them are fine for the quiet of your own home and include music (zombies are a constant muse for rock bands, it seems) and games of all kinds; others might involve stumbling out there amongst the other undead-loving hordes and getting involved in group activities from the slow and shuffling kind to the full-on running/jumping/fighting-off hordes variety. Which is surely what any gregarious gangrenous walker would want. Jump in to find out more....

Press Play

Oddly, the 1960s beat combo The Zombies are the one band with little or nothing to do with the undead. However, zombies and music have gone hand in hand for a long while, with some bands relying heavily on the 'undead' theme for both their music and stage shows.

As early as 1953, bands were incorporating zombies into their music, with examples including Lord Intruder's 'Zombie Jamboree' and the Crewnecks' 'Rockin' Zombie' in 1960.

'They're not dead exactly,
they're just…
sort of rotting.'

Lionel Cosgrove,
Braindead, 1992

Later references came from artists as diverse as Screamin' Jay Hawkins and Alice Cooper. However, the musical genre that really got its teeth into the zombie conceit was – perhaps inevitably – punk rock. What else would a musical style born of disenfranchisement and rejection of the norm do?

Punk and hard rock or metal acts to check out include White Zombie and the solo work of band member Rob Zombie (who also directed *House of 1000 Corpses*, 2003, and a reworked *Halloween*, 2007), plus a horde of 1980s punk acts recruited for the soundtrack of 1985's *Return of the Living Dead*, which included tracks from the Cramps ('Surfin' Dead') and the Damned ('Dead Beat Dance'). There are even the dubious joke-punk pleasures of Peter and the Test Tube Babies with 'Zombie Creeping Flesh', and, of course, the schlocky horror show of the Misfits.

Play On

More recently, a few outfits with a taste for the theatrical embraced the zombie look. Send More Paramedics' glorious splattergore rock was played in full rotting zombie makeup on stage (oddly, by day, one of them was a corporate lawyer); the band took their name from a line in *The Return of the Living Dead*. Going for a similar look but with a dark electro sound, Evil Nine (particularly on the album *They Live!*) brought a touch of death to the disco, while for a one-shot zombie tune, short-lived garage rock brats Be Your Own Pet's 'Crush!' will liven up any day, with its howled chorus of 'when there's no more room in heeeellllllll, the dead'll walk the Earrrrrth'.

Pawn
Carl's
Shotgun
Diaries
1/2010

HEATHE
THEATR

Of course there are many other potential additions to the zombie playlist so the zombie-loving muso should never go hungry for musical brains. While the Cranberries' famous track is an indictment of mindless, easily swayed mob mentality, it's not about 'zombies' *per se*; but how about electro punks Zombie Girl, with tunes including 'Jesus was a zombie'? Or the cataclysmic doomy gothica of The Horrors, whose 'Sheena is a Parasite' track features a video with Oscar nominee Samantha Morton spewing up her own intestines? So much music, so little time....

Getting Out More

You may have noticed, however, that zombies aren't generally known for loafing around the house playing their records. They will insist on getting out and about amongst the general population and causing mischief.

Perhaps in keeping with this *esprit de corpse*, the phenomenon of 'zombie walks' is on the rise. The first documented outbreak seems to have been in Sacramento, USA, in 2000 since then it has become something of a worldwide activity, with walks taking place from Australia to the UK. Zombie walks do as the name suggests: fans of the undead gather, usually in elaborate costume, and roam around in a shuffling moaning horde. There can be any number of reasons behind the walk, from a charity fundraiser to something more akin to a performance art piece; it might even be an advertising flashmob, or simply some fans of the zombie genre getting together for a rotten knees-up.

'There's nothing on the radio when you're dead / There's nothing at the movie show when you're dead / There's nowhere left for you to go when you're dead / Do the dead, yeah do the dead / Do the dead, surfin' dead.'

The Cramps,
'Surfin' Dead'

Other variations include zombie pub crawls (giving a different definition to 'dead drunk'), or for those who would rather flee zombies than be them, zombie runs are obstacle races in which runners tackle assault courses while being chased by undead hordes trying to stop them reaching the finish line. It seems zombism really can be incorporated into any kind of lifestyle.

Zom.com

For those who don't play well with others, or at least not outdoors, there are plenty of zombie-inspired toys – yes, toys – on the market, from movie tie-ins (*Shaun of the Dead*, *Planet Terror*) to more generic *Attack of the Living Dead* dolls (maybe don't give them to your two-year old niece just yet). If tabletop action is more your scene than being out on the town, there are board games for zombie fans too, including *Zombies!!!*, *Last Night on Earth*, *Zombie Survival: The Board Game* and even a tie-in with *The Walking Dead*.

And, of course, the internet is an infinite resource of zombie blogs, fan fiction, lists, criticism and general unruly madness. For something a little different, however, *Zomblogalypse* (www.zomblogalypse.com) is well worth a watch. An ongoing video blog, it tells the story of a small group of survivors battling a zombie outbreak and posting video updates, complete with an impressive degree of undead bashing, running and screaming. The concept was recently picked up at the Cannes film festival, so a big screen debut may well be on the cards.

And if you're still not sated? Turn to page 125 for further sources of zombie goodness, you brain-sucking loon.

Watch out!
They get you while you're sleeping!
Invasion of the Body Snatchers
A Robert H. Solo Production of A Philip Kaufman Film
"Invasion of the Body Snatchers"
Donald Sutherland · Brooke Adams · Leonard Nimoy
Jeff Goldblum • Veronica Cartwright
Screenplay by W.D. Richter, Based on the novel "The Body Snatchers" by Jack Finney
Produced by Robert H. Solo • Directed by Philip Kaufman • Color
United Artists
A Transamerica Company
Copyright © 1979 United Artists Corporation All rights reserved
FOREIGN STYLE C

What Does It Mean?

Of the many great things about zombies, their flexibility as a dramatic device must be one of the most potent (provided you can witness it from a safe, bite-free distance). Surely nothing is as adaptable in any genre as the zombie? If we choose, they can simply be agents of terror, deployed by bloodthirsty creatives to rattle our teeth in our skulls and send us skittering for safety behind the sofa. They're nothing more (or less) than movie monsters, plot drivers, things that go bump in the night and help keep the latex industry afloat.

Or … they can be something else. They can signify anything we want, and stand for all manner of things.

Metaphorical Monsters

So if they're not just unhelpfully persistent sleepwalkers with disease in their teeth, what are zombies? What are they *for*? As their significance is the subject of plenty of film criticism and popular debate we don't have the space to delve too deeply into it here – but perhaps we can investigate some of the broad ideas. It's what Shaun would want us to do down the Winchester, provided we don't use the 'Z' word.

Early zombie-like (oops, used it already) beings were reflections of the concerns of their time. While not explicitly undead creatures in the later Romero mould, the pod people of *Invasion of the Body Snatchers* (1956), for example, could be seen as representing the '50s paranoia of communism, the

'The monsters that rose from the dead, they are nothing compared to the ones we carry in our hearts.'

Max Brooks, World War Z

fear of the loss of identity in the face of an all-conquering ideology that was seen as a threat to Western democracy.

Ironically, that same democracy and the capitalism that accompanies it lies at the root of one potential reading of modern zombie flicks such as *Dawn of the Dead* and *Shaun of the Dead*. As the dead converge on shopping malls, without any conscious thought to drive them there, they embody an unthinking rapacious consumerism – we shop, therefore we are.

Slaves to the Wage

Meanwhile, the actions of the brainless, unthinking undead of *Shaun* … are paralleled with the similarly thoughtless routines of the living. Their mindless actions are designed to hold a mirror to our societies: the real zombies are us, standing in line at bus stops not speaking to one another, working repetitive service jobs (an idea also explored in the 1930s film *White Zombie*), treading the same paths in a circadian rhythm. In a peculiar way a zombie apocalypse might even save us, breaking the routine and sending us on new paths – hence the redemptive journeys of Shaun and Liz from tired automatons to resourceful, strong individuals.

Modern Mania

Because we bring our fears with us to horror tales, zombies also come to reflect our current preoccupations. The success of Max Brooks's *World War Z* novel may be down in part to his unsettling prognostications of how humanity might really react to a zombie apocalypse: as in, we'd react in the same way we react to everything else, with tanks and guns and panic and violence. We'd squabble with one another, put up walls and singularly fail to cooperate as a species. In a climate fuelled by fear of terrorist attacks, climate change and economic wretchedness, is it any wonder the notion of a global catastrophe resonates so strongly with the modern mindset?

The film adaptation – along with *28 Days Later*, *Resident Evil* and many others – also confronts us with a fear of contagion. Zombies are plague made flesh, they give a body and voice to our horror of the viruses and pathogens out there in the world that we normally can't see. Only this time, they also allow a pyrrhic hope – we might not be able to bash a disease's brains in, but doing just that to a zombie stand-in will make us feel better about it for a while.

天堂
天堂
さん
ますように

Born Free

Like *Dracula* before them (and vampires are a kind of zombie, after all), zombies may also point to a fear of the foreign or unknown. We fear what we do not understand – it's a trick that horror storytellers have employed for centuries – so when they arrive, seemingly from nowhere and with habits that are incomprehensible to us, our reaction is terror.

As they spread, we see the fall of free will before them. The zombie generally has no self-determination and is driven purely by hunger: they become at once our fear of the baser, more animalistic side of human nature and of losing our sentience and capacity to govern our own lives. And, also, we might not want to chow down on brains.

Zombies are all of these things and more. They're our demons, our distrust of other people, our worst flaws. And, of course, they're death. Death in physical form, roaming the streets in groaning surround sound. Even though they move slowly, clumsily (most of the time, anyway), we still do not seem able to get away from them – and so it is with death. It's gonna get us. Which can be a scary thought.

In other words, zombies are marvellous storytelling tools as well as being fall-down-and-whimper scary. The point often isn't the zombies themselves, it's how they make us act. There's no one rule for what they are: if we all thought the same, we'd just be a bunch of mindless – hang on....

Conclusion: The Z Factor

They're noisy, untidy, rotting, thoughtless and they want to eat us. Not exactly the ideal house guest, in other words. So why do zombies remain so appealing? What is it about the undead hordes that seems to have us coming back for more, despite knowing what we're in for?

With the possible exception of *Warm Bodies*, we can probably discount any kind of personal appeal. Unlike vampires, zombies are hardly sexy creatures and possess none of their dark, magnetic allure. But one thing they do share is fear: zombies, especially the latter-day world munching plague kind, are terrifying; and we like to be a little scared sometimes. It gets the pulse racing and reminds us we're alive.

Which may be another reason to be intrigued by Z. We dedicate our minds in every cultural sphere to the endeavour of understanding life, our mortality and our inevitable death. We ruminate on it in novels, prepare ourselves through faith and philosophy, sing about it, even illustrate it. Death appears in many incarnations throughout art, so perhaps the zombie is also an extension of this: a manifestation of death for us to gape at in horrid fascination.

End of the World as We Know It (and We Feel Fine)

As we gape, we might notice that zombies are extremely varied creatures throughout popular culture. They walk, shuffle, run – even dance – and come with astonishing appearances,

'Organise before they rise!'

Max Brooks,
The Zombie Survival Guide

whether it's the kohl-eyed undead of *Night of the Living Dead* or red-eyed rabid terrors of *28 Days Later*. They give artists a huge amount of licence to thrill, and they take it and run – contemporary zombie art shows lurid technicolour beasts alongside muted, desolate beings, and lets us peer into versions of our homes and cities we hope to never see: empty, overrun with foliage and littered with corpses (some of them walking).

We shouldn't forget that it's often the consequences of zombies, rather than the zombies themselves, that prove so intriguing. They let us play out human dramas against a backdrop of assured destruction, showing our recurring concerns in a whole new light and offering the chance to reassess what might be important. The end of the world is a great way to reflect on the human condition, and zombies are only too happy to provide a doomsday scenario.

In other words, zombies may be an enigma and a terror, but they're never dull. They entertain, yes, but also let us imagine, hope, fear and look within ourselves. Perhaps that's the great trick that zombies pull off to make us love them: by being dead, they teach us more about being alive. Which is probably worth a celebratory dance. Ready, set, shuffle....

'I have always liked the monster within idea. I like the zombies being us. Zombies are the blue-collar monsters.'

George A. Romero

More Braaiiiiins! Further Zombie Information

Books

Zombies! An Illustrated History of the Undead
by Jovanka Vucovic

Zombie Holocaust: How the Living Dead Devoured Pop Culture by David Flint

The Zombie Survival Guide: Recorded Attacks by Max Brooks

Zombies: A Record of the Year of Infection by Don Roff

Zombies Hate Stuff by Greg Stones

Fan Fiction

If you want to read, or create, home-brewed zombie tales head here …

homepageofthedead.com

talesofworldwarz.com

fanfiction.net (various zombie crossovers)

The Walking Dead

Choose your genre: comics or TV?

thewalkingdead.com (comics)

amctv.com/shows/the-walking-dead (TV series)

Authors

A few heavy hitters to investigate …

Max Brooks: maxbrooks.com

Stephen King: stephenking.com

Seth Grahame-Smith: sethgrahamesmith.com

Brian Keene: briankeene.com

Zombie Walks and Social Sites

Visit at your own risk!

crawlofthedead.com

terror4fun.com

Paquita Maria Sanchez: 'Your mother ate my dog!'

Lionel Cosgrove: 'Not all of it.'

Braindead, 1992

Acknowledgments

Biographies

Russ Thorne (Author)

If the zombie apocalypse arrives tomorrow, Russ Thorne hopes he'll be well prepared. A university career partially spent studying English but mainly watching Italian zombie video nasties late at night with his housemates should help, along with years of dedicated Romero viewing and getting red on himself. He's been known to dress up as the living dead on occasion too, sometimes even on purpose. When not stacking tins and bottled water in the basement he writes for the national press (including *The Independent* and *I*) and has previously written books on tattoo art, vampires and warriors. He lives in York, where there has been a known zombie problem for years, with his wife and dog – who are not known to be part of it.

Rosie Fletcher (Foreword)

Rosie is the Associate Editor of *Total Film*. She has written for a range of other publications including *Metal Hammer*, *Stylist*, *DVD Review*, *BAFTA*, and *Which?*. She is also a regular contributor of horror content to *SFX Magazine* and writes for their horror and zombies specials. Horror is her passion and during her career she has been turned into a zombie more than once.

Picture Credits

Special thanks to all the artists who have contributed artwork for this book, in page order: **© Joe Roberts** 1 & 21 & 95, 104; **© Przemysław Korczyński (Shamie)** 3 & 33 & 108; **© 2005 Aleksi Briclot and Benjamin Carré** 4; **© Chris Baginski** 6 & 120; **Corlen Kruger/© Atomhawk Design** 7 & 121, 66, 76; **© Aaron Sims** 8 & 128, 26; **© Alan Lathwell** 9 & 75; **© Misael Barbosa & Ricardo Marron** 10; **© Marcus Jones** 12 & 92; **© The Gurch** 15, 78, 82; **© Cloud Quinot** 16; **© Adam Howie** 18; **© Chris Shehan** 20 & 113; **© Eduardo Diaz** 24; **© Francis Tsai** 28, 127; **© Dave Oliver** 31 & 56; **© David Palumbo** 67 & 122; **© Dino Tomic** 69; **© Paul Alexandrescu** 70 & 93; **© Helen Norcott** 72; **© Andy Monks** 85, 86; **© Christopher Pigden (nedgip.com)** 88; **© Eydea Studios (eydeastudios.com)** 96; **© Henrik Sahlstrom** 98; **© Andrea Meloni** 100; **© Mike Penn** 103; **© Steve Argyle** 106; **© Rolf Bertz** 110; **© Shogun Rising/Noah Bradley** 114 & 118; **© Denis Kozionov** 124.

Courtesy of/© **Photoshot** (and the following): **LFI** 13, 37; **FOX SEARCHLIGHT PICTURES** 22; **Overbrook Entertainment** 30; **RKO Radio Pictures** 32; **Laurel Group/LFI 1978** 34; **Idols** 38, 58, 104; **Seven Arts Productions** 40; **NEW WORLD PICTURES/ Entertainment Pictures** 42; **Working Title Films** 43, 117; **New Line Cinema** 44; **Impact Pictures** 47, 91; **Screen Gems** 48; **Michael Gibson/Universal Studios/Entertainment Pictures** 50; **Summit Entertainment** 50; **Columbia Pictures** 52; **Paramount Pictures** 54; **Michael Gibson/Universal Pictures/ZUMA Press** 57; **Steve Wilkie** 60, 62; **UPPA** 64; **Orion Pictures** 81; **Sony Pictures/Entertainment Pictures/ ZUMAPRESS.com** 90; **The Legacy Collection/LFI** 112.